Legends of Rock & Roll

The Monkees

An unauthorized fan tribute

By: James Hoag

"Legends of Rock & Roll – The Monkees" Copyright 2014 James Hoag. All rights reserved. Manufactured in the United States of America. No parts of this book may be reproduced in any form or by any electronic or mechanical means including information storage and retrieval systems without written permission from the publisher. The only exception is for a reviewer. A reviewer may quote brief passages in a review. Published by www.number1project.com Monument Marketing Publishing LTD., 53 Hanover Dr., Orem, Utah 84058

Paperback Edition

Other Paperbacks by James Hoag

Legends of Rock and Roll Series

Legends of Rock & Roll Volume 1 - The Fifties

Legends of Rock & Roll Volume 2 - The Sixties

Legends of Rock & Roll Volume 3 - The Seventies

The Beatles, Queen

Individual Beatles

John Lennon, Paul McCartney, George Harrison,

Ringo Starr

Fifties

Everly Brothers

Sixties

Neil Diamond, Roy Orbison, The Beach Boys,

Bob Dylan, The Doors, The Bee Gees,

The Grateful Dead, Simon & Garfunkel, The Monkees

The Four Seasons

Seventies

Eagles, Bruce Springsteen

Eighties

Madonna

Legends of Country Music

Reba McEntire, Willie Nelson, Johnny Cash,

George Jones, Merle Haggard, Garth Brooks,

Waylon Jennings

(All Available at Amazon.com)

James Hoag

Table of Contents

Introduction	7
In the Beginning	9
Micky Dolenz	12
Davy Jones	15
Peter Tork	18
Michael Nesmith	20
The Coming Together of the Monkees	23
Tommy Boyce & Bobby Hart	25
The Pilot	27
Becoming a Real Band	30
"Last Train to Clarksville"	32
The First Album "*The Monkees*"	34
"I'm a Believer"	37
The Reverse British Invasion	39
"Headquarters"	43
"Pleasant Valley Sunday"	46
"Daydream Believer"	49

A House of Cards	51
"The Birds, The Bees & The Monkees"	54
"Head"	57
"33 1/3 Revolutions per Monkee"	60
The In-Between Years	63
MTV Revives The Monkees	67
"Justus"	71
One Last Tour	73
The Loss of Davy Jones	74
Legacy of The Monkees	77
Afterword	78
About the Author	80
Selected Discography	81
Episode List	83

INTRODUCTION

"Hey, Hey, We're the Monkees!" Who doesn't remember those famous words? At least if you were alive in the Sixties, you probably remember them.

I absolutely loved the Monkees. The music was great, but I really liked the television show. With this group, you had the best of both worlds. It's probably no secret that the Monkees were a "manufactured" band. They were four guys that were chosen especially for the show. They were, and are today, Micky Dolenz, who played drums, Davy Jones, who sang and played percussion (Davy died in 2012, more about this later,) Peter Tork, who played guitar (Peter died in 2019 after a ten-year battle with cancer,) and Michael Nesmith, who was the lead guitarist. They were literally created by two guys who wanted to put together a group that would be the American equivalent of the Beatles.

The Beatles were the hottest band in the world in the Sixties, and America needed an answer to that. The Monkees never came up to the level of the Beatles, but they were fun and, even though they were created from nothing, they had talent.

If it had been just bad music, no one would have bought it; but they were really good. I had just gotten married when the Monkees came on the scene, and I can remember rocking my new baby and listening to the Monkees on the radio. We were in Dallas, away from home, and the Monkees helped brighten the day when we were feeling homesick.

Be warned, however; this is kind of a sad story. Life was good for the Monkees some of the time, but much of the time there was conflict and sorrow. Here we have four guys who were never really friends trying to get along with one another and sometimes succeeding and sometimes failing.

Lovingly called the Pre-Fab Four, here are the Monkees.

IN THE BEGINNING

I'm going to turn things around a little. If you've read any of my other books, you know I usually start with a brief history of the life of the performer before they became famous. But in this case, I'd like to start with the creation of the group and how they came to be.

The Monkees really started on February 6, 1964. That's the famous day the Beatles appeared for the first time in America and performed on *The Ed Sullivan Show*. Each of the four guys who would later become the Monkees were watching that night and, like so many other performers of the Sixties, it inspired them. They each felt that they could do what the Beatles were doing and they hadn't even met each other yet.

Later that summer, the Beatles would release their first movie, *A Hard Day's Night* to great acclaim. It debuted in England first and then came to America in August. This did not escape the notice of two producers in Hollywood who had been thinking of creating a television show about musicians who were a lot like the Beatles.

Bert Schneider and Bob Rafelson had just created a new company called Raybert Productions and were looking for a project to promote to the television networks. Rafelson had had some experience with other television shows. He had worked on *The Wackiest Ship in the Army*, a show based on the movie of the same name in New York. It was after being fired from the show and retreating to the West Coast that he met Bert Schneider.

The appeal of *A Hard Day's Night* told Bert Schneider and Bob Rafelson that it was doable and they set about to put together a show which featured silly musicians having all sorts of fun and misadventures. They now thought they had a good chance of selling the idea to a television network. This would be really the first show that showed young people as the main characters. I looked through a list of television shows that were playing in 1966 and none of them featured just young people. *Batman* had his Robin and the *Adams Family* had children, but there were always adults around to supervise.

Rafelson wanted a show that would star just the young rock stars and show their antics as they went from one silly situation to another. For Rafelson, the idea goes back to before the Beatles were even known. He had the idea of doing a show like this years before, only the group would be a folk group who travelled around having adventures. He had never been able to get anything off the ground until the Beatles came along and proved it could be done. The country was ripe for a show about rock and roll.

They needed financing, and they needed a name. They tossed around many names (including, believe it not, *The Creeps*), but finally settled on *The Monkees* with its odd spelling to set it apart. Screen Gems was the television arm of Columbia Pictures, so they went to the head of Screen Gems who, at the time, was Jackie Cooper. Cooper had been in Hollywood all of his life, being a child star starting at the age of three. He agreed to bankroll the show to the tune of $250,000.

It looked like they were on their way. Everything seemed to be falling into place. Oh, did I mention that Bert Schneider's father, Abe Schneider, was the president of Columbia Pictures? They say that didn't influence things, but the old saying goes; "it's all in who you know." They had their idea, they had the money. Now, they just needed a cast.

They auditioned a couple of bands who were already recording at the time. They talked to the Dave Clark Five who had many hits on the tails of the Beatles and were definitely part of the British Invasion, but they didn't seem right. They also talked to the Lovin' Spoonful who were at least American and just coming up in 1966, but John Sebastian had signed over the music rights of his band to another company and

Screen Gems wouldn't be able to market their music without a big legal hassle, so they were dropped.

Thus, they ended up sending out a casting call for players in their drama. From September 8 - 10, 1966 *Daily Variety* and *The Hollywood Reporter* ran an ad asking for boys to come audition: "Running parts for 4 insane boys, age 17-21," the ad read. Over 400 young men came to audition. Of some of the people you might have heard of who tried out for the Monkees were Paul Williams and Harry Nilsson, both of whom would go on to big careers of their own. Nilsson would have eight Top 40 songs starting in 1969 including the number one "Without You."

Probably the most famous of the people who auditioned was Steven Stills, who was, at the time, a member of Buffalo Springfield and had a Top 10 song with "For What it's Worth (Stop, Hey What's That Sound)," but Stills didn't fit the image they wanted for the group. One thing Stills did do that was important: he recommended a friend of his named Peter Tork.

Actually, people would like to think that the four boys were selected from the 400 who auditioned but, in fact, just one was: Michael Nesmith. Davy Jones was already under contract with Screen Gems and had show business experience. He was a shoe-in right from the beginning. Peter was recommended by Steven Stills, and Micky was told by his agent to go audition. Only Michael of the four came because he saw the advertisement.

Now that we have the four guys assembled, let's go back and see how they got to this point.

MICKY DOLENZ

Let's start with Micky. He became the drummer and one of the lead singers of the Monkees. Micky was born George Michael Dolenz on March 5, 1945 at the Cedars of Lebanon Hospital in Los Angeles, California. I'm pretty sure he was named after his father, but the family would call him Micky. His parents were George Dolenz and Janelle Johnson.

He had three sisters growing up, all of which went into some form of show business. Coco, born Gemma Maria in 1949, would have a brief career in show business. Younger sisters were Deborah, born in 1958, and Kathleen (called "Gina") born in 1960.

Micky came about his talent naturally, being the son of George Dolenz. George was a professional actor who had many credits to his name by the time Micky grew up. His most noteworthy accomplishment was being the star of a television series which ran for 39 episodes in 1956 called *The Count of Monte Cristo*. He started acting in 1941 and has 44 credits to his name according to imdb.com. His final role was in the show *Bonanza* in 1963 just before he died.

Micky's mother was Janelle Johnson Dolenz who acted under the name of Janelle Johnson. She appeared in two films in the Forties, neither of which look that significant to me. They were *Since You Went Away* (1944) and *The Brute Man* (1946). It appears after marrying George, she gave up her life as an actor.

At the same time that his father was appearing in *The Count of Monte Cristo*, Micky was also acting in a television show in 1956. He starred in a children's show, first on NBC and then on ABC, called *Circus Boy* in which he played an orphaned water boy named Corky who took care of Bimbo the elephant. His parents, the Flying Falcons, were tragically killed in a circus accident, leaving him an orphan. He was taken in by Joey the clown, played by Noah Berry, Jr. He acted under the name of Micky Braddock (I've also seen it spelled with an 'e': Mickey) but now every reference you find about the show gives his real name. The show ran for just two seasons.

The important thing about this job was, it was Micky's first exposure to acting and the acting life (he was eleven at the time) and even more important, they sent him on tour with Bimbo, the elephant and required him to sit on the elephant and strum a guitar and sing a little to Bimbo. As a result, Micky was sent to school to learn to play the guitar and to learn some fundamental singing.

If I had grown up in the Fifties in L.A., I might have tried to get into films and televisions shows, too. By the time he graduated from High School, he had played in three different series, usually just bit parts. In 1958, he played in an episode of *Zane Grey Theater*, but the credits still read Micky Braddock. Then the next year, again as Braddock, he played in an episode of *Playhouse 90*, where his fellow actors included Art Carney and Leslie Nielsen.

Micky graduated from Ulysses S Grant High School in Valley Glen, Los Angeles in 1962. Grant High School, being in Los Angeles, you would expect it to graduate a lot of people of whom you might have heard. Actually, the list is quite long, but the most famous one I saw was Tom Selleck who graduated the same year Micky did: 1962. I don't know if they were friends. After high school, he played with several bands including his own band "Micky and the One Nighters." He actually recorded a record as part of this band, but it never did anything.

A couple of years later, in 1964, he got a role in the TV show *Mr. Novak*. Frankly, I hadn't thought of this show in at least 50 years but in the mid-Sixties, this was one of my favorite programs. Now, I don't remember Micky being on the show but then no one knew who he was at this point anyway, but I really loved *Mr. Novak*.

After that, he played (uncredited) in three episodes of *Peyton Place* and then in 1965, his manager mentioned this audition that would change his life forever. Micky joined 400+ other young boys who auditioned for a part on the new show *The Monkees*. He auditioned by playing the Chuck Berry standard, "Johnny B. Goode." I don't have to tell you that he won the part.

Yes, he won the part, but one reason he won was his aggressiveness during the audition. When he came into the office of Schneider and Rafelson, the place was a mess. There were pizza boxes and coke cans all over the floor and the guys were intent on staking a pile of coke cans and cartons as high as they could. Micky reached over and placed a can on the top of the pile and yelled "Checkmate." I think this did more than anything to insure him a place on the team.

DAVY JONES

For some reason, I always believed that Davy Jones was a stage name and surely he was born with a different name, but not so. Davy was born David Thomas Jones on December 30, 1945. He is the only Brit in the group, being born in Manchester, England. His father was Harry Jones and, I believe, an engineer for British Rail. British Rail provided the majority of public transportation for Britain from about 1948 until the mid-Nineties when the company was privatized. So, I assume Dad Harry was gone a lot. He died of emphysema in 1969, so he did get a chance to see his son as a Monkee.

His mother was Doris Jones and was a homemaker all of her life. She, unfortunately, didn't get to see Davy become a Monkee, dying in 1960 of the same disease that later killed her husband, emphysema. Davy was thirteen at the time and understandably devastated. Davy had three sisters, the same number as Micky. Their names were Hazel, Beryl, and Lynda.

Davy was always a small boy. As an adult, he topped out at five foot three inches tall. Being of a short stature, his father thought he would make a good jockey and sent him to a local racetrack to learn the craft. He started training under the tutelage of Basil Foster. Foster would almost become a father figure to Davy and was his friend for the rest of his life.

Some say that David hated racing and horses and took the first chance he got to get away from it, but I think he loved the equestrian life. Later in life, after the Monkees was over, he actually got his jockey's license in Pennsylvania. I've seen many pictures of Davy with horses, and he looks happy.

Foster is sort of responsible for him getting into acting, however. A theater in London's East End needed a small person for a part and asked Foster if he knew anyone. He knew how charismatic Davy was and recommended him. He got the part and left horse racing behind forever. From there, he got a role in a soap opera named *Coronation Street*. He had a small part on just one episode, but it was enough that he got the bug.

Next, he auditioned for and got the part of the Artful Dodger in the London performances of *Oliver!* For this role, he won national acclaim, and he was on his way. *Oliver!* played in London for a while and then moved to New York on Broadway. Davy was able to come with it. He was nominated for a Tony Award for Best-Supporting Actor in a musical for his role in 1963.

If you're old enough to remember the *Ed Sullivan Show* (I am), then you might remember that he would feature scenes from Broadway plays to advertise them and to entertain the audience. Sullivan arranged to have a scene from *Oliver!* portrayed on the show. The night scheduled for this was February 9, 1964. As already mentioned, that was the night The Beatles appeared on the *Ed Sullivan Show* for the very first time.

What's remarkable is that Davy Jones was in the wings waiting his turn to appear on Sullivan and was able to watch the entire Beatles' performance. This is what I call a moment in music history. Here we have the Beatles and just a few feet away stands the boy who would later become famous himself because of the Beatles. Without the Beatles, the Monkees might never have happened.

Like so many young men in the early Sixties, the Beatles inspired Davy to continue his career. He literally looked at the Beatles and said to himself, "I want a piece of that." And, of course, he got it.

Between Ed Sullivan and the Monkees, Davy stayed in the states and in 1965 signed a contract with Screen Gems, the company that would eventually produce the TV show. While he was waiting for the Monkees to happen (of course, he didn't know what was about to happen), he took roles in other television shows. He had a role in a *Ben Casey* episode, a TV doctor show that ran from 1961 until 1966 and starred Vince Edwards, and also in an episode of a show called *The Farmer's Daughter*.

Davy did have to audition for the part in the Monkees, but it was only a formality. Rafelson didn't like him at first. He didn't think Davy could really get into the part. Time would prove him wrong, of course. He couldn't really sing that well, but that came with time. His biggest asset was something he could really do nothing about, his British accent. The team wanted to complete with the Beatles. How better to do it than with another Brit.

Needless to say, he was hired.

PETER TORK

Peter was born Peter Halsten Thorkelson on February 13, 1942 in Washington D.C. His mother was Virginia Hope (Straus) and his father was Halsten John Thorkelson (everyone called him John) and was an economics professor. Peter had a sister, Anne, and two brothers, Nick and Christopher.

His early life sounds kind of chaotic. Born in D.C, he moved to Detroit, Michigan and then to Berlin, Germany, then on to Wisconsin before finally stopping and settling in Connecticut. Almost from the beginning, Peter showed an interest and an aptitude for music. He is the only one of the four who came to the Monkees already knowing how to play various instruments. He started with the piano when he was nine and by the time he graduated from High School, he knew how to play the banjo and the guitar and several other instruments. He eventually played guitar, electric guitar, banjo, keyboards, piano, organ, French horn, bass, and ukulele for the Monkees. But this was only after convincing the producers and others he could actually play the instruments.

After graduating from college, Peter went to Carleton College in Northfield, Minnesota from 1960 until 1963, but ended up failing and having to leave. Peter, himself, said that one of his problems was that he had an inferiority complex. Also, it didn't help that he had gotten married to a woman named Jody Babb in June of 1960. The marriage lasted less than a year, and they were divorced in September of 1960. Consequently, he made his way to New York City where he decided to use his talent with various instruments to try to obtain work in Greenwich Village.

It was about this time that he started shortening his name and just went by Peter Tork. It was easier to pronounce and easier to remember. He spent a couple years bumming around Greenwich Village, playing the different clubs. He met up with Stephen Stills in the Village and the two were part of a band called Buffalo Fish. That didn't last long, but Peter and Stills became lifelong friends because of it. Buffalo Fish would go on to become Buffalo Springfield, but Peter had left the group by this time.

As already mentioned, when Stills auditioned for the Monkees and was turned down, he recommended Peter as a good fit. Thus, Peter made his way to the West Coast and auditioned himself. He was just what they were looking for. His inferiority complex gave him a shy, withdrawn demeanor and the producers liked that contrast with the other three members.

We now have three of the four together. Let's see what Michael was doing.

MICHAEL NESMITH

Michael was born Robert Michael Nesmith on December 30, 1942 in Houston, Texas. His parents were Warren Audrey and Bette Nesmith. Michael's story is very similar to my own. His father went off to fight in World War II as did mine. When he came back, the couple decided they could not be married any longer and so divorced in 1946. Michael was born while his Dad was gone fighting. All of this would also apply to me. However, from this point forward, it is much different.

Bette moved to Dallas, Texas after the divorce and began life as a single mother of one young boy. Her story is almost as interesting as Michael's. She became a secretary and worked at Texas Bank and Trust. This was the day of electric typewriters and, unlike computers, where you can backspace and make a correction if you make a mistake, when you made a mistake on a typewriter, you either left it or started over again.

Bette had had some experience in graphic design and knew that when a painter made a mistake, he just painted over it and started again. She thought, *"Why not do the same thing on a typewriter?"* So, with the aid of her son's chemistry set, she invented a white liquid that could be spread on paper to cover up mistakes. This evolved into what we know today as Liquid Paper (or "White Out"). In 1979, she sold the company to Gillette Corporation for $47.5 million.

I think this explains a lot of the way Michael treated the rest of the band after the Monkees broke up.

Michael was a creative student. In his younger days, he wrote poetry and participated in choral groups and when he was fifteen, he enrolled in the Dallas Theater Center teen program. He was indifferent to school, however, and never finished high school. In 1960, he dropped out and joined the Air Force. He did his basic training at Lackland

AFB in San Antonio, Texas. I find this interesting because I joined the Air Force in 1960 and also went to Lackland. That was where basic training was held in those days. The thought that I might have been on the base at the same time as Michael Nesmith is very intriguing to me.

When Michael was nineteen years old, he bought a guitar. He had never taken a guitar lesson; he was completely self-taught. This was the first time in his life that he had even thought about music, but the creative side of him began to come out again and he started writing songs. He got together with a guy named John Kuehne (professionally, he went by the name John London) and the two worked together on original songs and performances, calling themselves "Mike & John." Michael worked under the name of Michael Blessing. Kuehne would later become important to Michael after the Monkees. He also met a girl named Phyllis Ann Barbour and in 1963, they were married. By now, he was playing and writing regularly and so the couple decided to move to California so they could be "where the action was." John London went with them.

In Los Angeles, he played the clubs and got what work he could. Phyllis was pregnant and would eventually give birth to Michael's first son, Christian DuVal, who was born on January 31, 1965. Michael billed himself as a folk singer and took part in the hootenannies which occurred every Monday night at The Troubadour, a night club in West Hollywood. He met Randy Sparks of The New Christie Minstrels and began publishing songs for him.

Songs that came out of his relationship with Sparks were "Mary Mary" which Michael wrote for the Paul Butterfield Blues Band. He also wrote "Different Drum" which was a big hit for Linda Ronstadt and the Stone Poneys in 1968 and peaked at number thirteen. This was Ronstadt's first hit before she went solo. She also recorded "Some of Shelly's Blues" which Michael wrote and this song has a real country sound to it. It should have charted on the country charts, but it didn't.

He also wrote "Pretty Little Princess" for Frankie Laine who recorded it in 1968. Another nice song that has a country feel to it. So Michael was having some success but not really taking over the music world.

It was during this time period (late 1965) that he heard about auditions for a new television show. Michael, thinking he could get a job as a song writer, applied for the job. He appeared at the audition with his guitar to show to them that he could sing and play and, surprisingly, wore a wool cap. The cap surprised Schneider and Rafelson and they liked it. They liked Michael and forever more he would be known by one of his nicknames, "Wool Hat."

A few other nicknames Michael is known as is Nez or Papa Nez. He would pick this up later from his fans.

The Coming Together of the Monkees

Davy Jones was, by far, the audience favorite of those who saw the auditions, but he wasn't accepted right away. Schneider and Rafelson whittled the applicants down to eight guys and from those eight, they choose the final four: Davy, Michael, Peter, and Micky. They had two musicians and two actors.

Of course, screen tests were done by everyone who applied for the job. Some of those screen tests actually made it into some of the televised shows. Rafelson was putting together four distinct individuals who had the misfortune of having never worked together before. Every other group that I have written about came up through the ranks and molded themselves into what you eventually heard on a record.

The Monkees were a completely unknown quantity. Peter and Michael had met before since they had both worked the same folk circuit in Los Angeles, but it would be a stretch to say that they were friends. No one really knew anyone else. Part of getting the show off the ground was to get them to work together and appear, at least on screen, as a cohesive unit.

Micky and Davy came together first. They were both actors and had been in the business and bonded together to some extent. Peter and Michael felt like outsiders, and it was harder for them to be accepted but, eventually, they were. Michael later said that the Monkees were never "all for one and one for all." They were always four distinct individuals. But, he said, he believes that is what made it work.

Unfortunately, they really didn't get along too well right at the beginning. Four boys ranging in age from nineteen (Davy) to twenty-three (Peter) made for some friction between the guys. On one of the first days of filming, the guys actually got into a food fight in the cafeteria of the Screen Gems.

Don Kirshner, who was a music publisher with Screen Gems and who would later have a big influence on the band, was put in charge of the music for the show. He heard some of the songs that Tommy Boyce and Bobby Hart had written and recommended them to Bert Schneider for the show. Schneider, taking the advice of Kirshner, hired Boyce and Hart, to write the music for the show.

TOMMY BOYCE & BOBBY HART

This is not a book about Boyce and Hart, but you can't discuss the Monkees and not include them. They had a profound effect on the group. Both guys had had success as singers, but it was as songwriters that they really shined. Boyce wrote one of his first songs for Fats Domino. "Be My Guest" was a big hit for Fats in 1959.

Boyce met Bobby Hart in 1959, and the two would work together for many years. They had little success, however, until 1964 when they wrote "Lazy Elsie Molly" for Chubby Checker, a minor hit for him. Then they wrote "Come a Little Bit Closer" for Jay & the Americans which was a number three hit in 1964. Now people were starting to pay attention to them. They wrote "(I'm Not Your) Steppin' Stone" for Paul Revere and the Raiders in 1966, but it didn't chart for them, so they gave the song to the Monkees, and they had a number twenty hit with it.

Even while working for the Monkees, Boyce and Hart would record their own music. In 1967, they had a minor hit, just breaking into the Top 40 at number 39 with "Out & About." Then in 1968, they had a hit that most people remember: "I Wonder What She's Doing Tonight," a song I really like. It peaked at number eight, which was their only Top 10 song. Then, later in 1968, they hit the Top 40 again with "Alice Long (You're My Favorite Girlfriend)" which made it to number twenty seven.

Boyce and Hart had a good career, but things dropped off after the Monkees. They kept things going for a few years and eventually went their own ways and formed their own bands. But things were never the same as they had been during the late Sixties. In 1994, Tommy Boyce returned to Nashville, and there suffered with depression and a brain aneurysm. He took his own life on November 23, 1994. Bobby Hart still lives with his wife in Los Angeles.

Boyce and Hart were commissioned to write, at first, three songs for the upcoming television show. They started with "(Theme from) the Monkees," "I Wanna Be Free," and "Let's Dance On" all of which appear on the pilot episode.

These songs were written even before the cast had been decided on. In fact, Boyce and Hart wanted to be part of the cast but didn't make it. They wrote the entire score for the pilot. During the filming of the pilot episode, it was actually Boyce and Hart that did the singing and the actors just lip synced to the songs. Fortunately, when the show eventually aired, the actual Monkees did the singing as their voices were dubbed in over the top of the original Boyce and Hart vocals. B&H did continue to write for the show for most of the first season.

THE PILOT

When the pilot was taped, the guys had never played together. They couldn't be depended on to act as a cohesive unit so allowances had to be made. As much as the guys wanted to sing and play their own stuff, the producers couldn't take the chance until they proved themselves. When the pilot was played for test audiences, they hated it. If you watch the pilot on YouTube, you'll see a couple clips that show the original auditions before a decision was made as to who, exactly, would be the Monkees. These are now placed at the end of the show. When the show was played again for a second test audience, they put those auditions at the beginning of the show and that seemed to help a lot. The second test audience liked the show much better than the first one did.

NBC decided to take a chance and green lighted the show for a complete season.

I just watched the pilot (it's on YouTube, like everything else), and it's funny. It's called "Here Come the Monkees," and it involves the boys acting silly while Davy is infatuated with a girl. I am probably showing my age, but I remember watching *The Monkees* when it was first aired. I didn't think of it at the time, but these guys remind me of The Three Stooges. Then I read that to prepare for the show, the studio had them watch Marx Brothers' and Three Stooges' movies, so my impression was right on. Monkee fans might hate me for saying that, but the slapstick comedy is very similar, just brought up to date (to the Sixties) and aimed directly at a teenage audience.

The show looked like it was totally improvised. It took a lot of work to achieve that impression. What you notice first about *The Monkees* show which you didn't see in other TV shows was the sudden and frequent changes of costume. They would be telling one story line and suddenly they were wearing completely different costumes and acting out some little mini-play within the main story. A normal 30 minute situation comedy show would have in the neighborhood of twenty five or so set-ups. *The Monkees* used about 90. If you could keep up with it, it was great.

There were adults in the show, but they all acted like they had no control over the boys (which, of course, they didn't.) It was the first time a major television show had been produced around young people. There was no authority figure in the show and, therefore, chaos ensues and hilarity results. If you watch the singing closely, you can spot the fact that they are lip syncing the words. My favorite spot in the show was when the guys are in their home, and Michael throws a dart at a picture of the Beatles. I thought that said a lot about the group. Still, it's an entertaining half hour and I enjoyed it even in this, the twenty-first century.

The boys were portrayed as regular guys who seemed to get in a lot of trouble. They were certainly not rock stars and didn't act like stars. They were just young guys having fun and, in that premise, was the success of the show.

This pilot episode ended up being played as the actual tenth episode during the airing of the program. This was the only episode where a "manager" appeared. The manager, played by Bing Russell, was never seen again in the show.

James Frawley was hired to be the director of the first few shows. Frawley was another young guy without a lot of experience. However, he had done a lot of work in improvisation and had worked on two experimental films prior to coming to *The Monkees*. Once the pilot was shot, and they knew what they were dealing with, they took the boys and locked them away for six weeks to try to teach them to be actors. Frawley taught them to improvise and to work together and to be spontaneous. This was exactly the feel they wanted out of the show.

It wasn't all good, however. Training them to be spontaneous proved to leak out into their public lives. The boys couldn't turn it off. Whenever the studio had them out in public, chaos resulted. At one particular restaurant, Chasens in West Hollywood, in which NBC wanted to introduce the guys to potential sponsors, they kind of went nuts. There was a stuffed doll of the NBC peacock, and the boys played volleyball with it in the street in front of the restaurant. Micky found the fuse box for the restaurant and turned off all of the power. Other shenanigans resulted, and NBC, and especially the sponsors, were not amused. Several of them said, no way am I supporting this nonsense. Several television stations, when they heard about the incident, refused to broadcast *The Monkees*.

The show definitely got off to a rocky start. It had its fans, but it also had a lot of people who really hated it. *The Monkees*, as a television show, would only last two seasons and never broke the Top 25 shows on the television ratings list.

BECOMING A REAL BAND

The biggest problem with getting a show like this off the ground was that you had four guys who wanted to be a band but had never played as a band. Every other group that you can name came up through the ranks the hard way. There are very few overnight successes in the music business (except maybe, *American Idol*). The guys had to play like a band, and they had to act like they were one unit and that usually took years of work to get right. The Monkees had to do it right from the beginning.

In fact, at first, they didn't even know who would play which instrument. No one wanted to play the drums. Davy was the only one of the four who knew how to play and the producers felt he was so short, that he would get lost back there behind all the drum equipment, so Micky stepped up and volunteered to take the bullet and be the drummer. In the beginning, he didn't even know how to play. He spent much of the first season learning the craft.

The two who were actually musicians, Peter and Michael, were frustrated that they weren't able to play like they wanted to. The producers expected the guys to just stand by while everything else was done by other people. They had another big problem; Boyce and Hart had written songs for the pilot but now they needed songs for every episode. Someone had to write two or three new songs each week as the filming of the episodes continued. Kirshner asked Tommy Boyce and Bobby Hart to suggest five names of people they thought could do the job. They came up with the names: Boyce and Hart, Hart and Boyce, Tommy and Bobby, Bobby and Tommy, and TB & BH, but Kirshner just laughed at them.

Kirshner had brought in several different writers and music producers, but nothing had clicked yet. A fellow named Snuff Garrett, who had written songs for Gary Lewis and the Playboys, tried but the guys didn't like him and so he left. He asked Mickey Most (who had worked with the Animals and Herman's Hermits, among others), but Most said no. He then asked Carole King to give it a try. King spent one day in the studio with the guys and left in tears.

Finally, in desperation, Kirshner went back to the two who he had talked to in the first place: Boyce and Hart, and they were hired on a more full time basis. This was not an easy job. Writing music on a time table was difficult, and it took a particular kind of talent to do it. However, Boyce and Hart kept up with the show, writing new music as it was needed. They put together a band called the Candy Store Prophets who were professional musicians and whose purpose was to play the Monkees' music, so the real Monkees could lip sync to it.

The Candy Store Prophets consisted of Boyce, Hart, and three others: Gerry McGee on guitar (he would later play with a version of the band The Ventures of "Walk, Don't Run" fame), Larry Taylor on bass (he would later go on to play with Canned Heat) and Billy Lewis on Drums. Also playing as part of the Prophets was Lewis Shelton on guitar. He was good on the flamingo guitar and on at least one song, "Valleri," it is him playing when in the video, it looks like it is Michael Nesmith playing.

But the Monkees weren't about to be relegated to the back seat when it came to providing the music for the show. They needed to be able to play together and work together. After all, they had started out as four strangers that had had to become friends almost overnight.

Rafelson and Schneider really never thought they could become a truly functioning band, and the boys were determined to prove them wrong. Thus, in their spare time, they practiced together. Some say they had a sort of "garage band" sound that was not real good but not bad either. As they continued to work, they became better and better.

"Last Train to Clarksville"

When it came time to produce their first record, they needed a label. Kirshner arranged with RCA Victor to create a brand new label just for the Monkees, called Colgems (I'm assuming that it is a combination of Columbia and Screen Gems for which Kirshner worked.)

The first record released by the Monkees was "Last Train to Clarksville," written, of course, by Boyce and Hart. The flip side was "Take a Giant Step," and the record was released in August of 1966, just a month or so before the debut of the television show. It skyrocketed to number one on the Billboard charts. It also reached number twenty three in the United Kingdom. England was listening to the Monkees, also. Listen to "Last Train to Clarksville" and you'll hear hints of the Beatles' song "Paperback Writer." Bobby Hart heard the Beatles on the radio and liked the guitar intro to the song. He heard the first word of the song "Paperback" and what he heard in his mind was "take the last," just those words, and the song was built from there.

The song is about Clarksville, Tennessee which is right across the state line from Fort Campbell, Kentucky, the home of the 101th Airborne Division who served in the Vietnam War. The boy singing is about to leave for duty and wants one more night with his girl before he leaves because he doesn't know if he will ever be coming back.

The first episode of the Monkees was broadcast on September 12, 1966 and almost immediately, NBC and Columbia knew they had a hit on their hands, although maybe not as strong a hit as they would have liked. The first episode was called "Royal Flush" and, of course, involved Davy trying to get acquainted with a girl, this time a princess who he meets on the beach.

The four guys gathered at Schneider's home to watch the first episode. Everyone was nervous. How would it be received? Would it lay a big egg? Well, yes and no. The show was up against one of the most popular shows on television at the time, *Gilligan's Island,* and that show appealed to young people, also. Then there was the problem of only 160 stations of a possible 200 that actually aired the show. The stations were still upset over the mess the guys had made back at Chasens restaurant.

The ratings weren't great, but the critics liked the show. They were, of course, compared to the Beatles. But where the Beatles' humor was English, more subtle and dry, the Monkees' was all American. Their humor was almost slapstick. They were called the young Marx Brothers.

Some say it was not cool to like the Monkees, but I did. It never entered my mind that they were anything but cool. I didn't realize that they might not be playing the instruments that we heard on the television show. I guess I'm somewhat naïve when it comes to things like that, I accept what I see as the truth, not thinking about the things that might be going on in the background. As far as I was concerned, the Monkees were the American Beatles (the "Pre-Fab Four") and that was that.

However, it seems that it was uncool to like the Monkees. The show struggled for acceptance all during its two year run. Many years later, on the television show, *The Simpsons*, Marge admits that she liked the Monkees and seems ashamed of it. Her psychologist says "The Monkees weren't about music, Marge. They were about rebellion, about political and social upheaval." Well, I'm not so sure about that. For me, it was all about the music.

The First Album "*The Monkees*"

About a month after the release of "Last Train to Clarksville," Colgems released the first Monkees album simply titled *The Monkees* in October of 1966. It was on the Colgems label in the U.S. and on the RCA label in the rest of the world. The album would go to number one in the United States and England. It stayed at number one for thirteen weeks in the U.S. and only fell out when the group's second album took over the top spot. It spent a total of 78 weeks on the Billboard album charts, exactly a year and a half.

"Last Train to Clarksville" was the only hit single from the album, but the album included the title song from the television show and several other very interesting songs. What I find remarkable is that none of the actual Monkees played on that first album. All of the music on the album except for one track was provided by members of Candy Store Prophets, Boyce and Hart's session group. If you check the track listing, you'll see that Micky Dolenz and Davy Jones are listed as lead singers on different tracks. The only exception is "Papa Gene's Blues" which was written by Michael Nesmith and he sings lead vocal on the song. Peter also plays on the song, but that is the only song on the album that Peter is listed as even a participant.

Also, Michael co-wrote and sings on "Sweet Young Thing" which includes a young musician named Glen Campbell who was playing session work before he became famous himself. Most of the songs are written by Boyce and Hart, but there a couple of exceptions. I've mentioned those that were written by Michael. There were two songs written or co-written by Gerry Goffin (the husband of Carole King) and one written by David Gates who would later become the lead singer of the Seventies group Bread.

So, without hardly playing a note, the Monkees had a number one album and were known worldwide. Later, in the mid-Eighties, when MTV would bring back the Monkees, the album would spend another twenty four weeks on the album charts. For a band with little respect, they were doing pretty good.

The schedule was grueling. They were actors, and they were musicians. Few bands had to perform both roles. They would be in the studio filming for up to twelve hours a day and then they tried to practice the instruments and become a cohesive unit as a regular band. In December of 1966, they went on their first live tour. Here was an opportunity to show what they could really do. You can't fake it when you're playing live. Well, not entirely, anyway. The Candy Store Prophets went along and played backup for the tour, just in case they needed a little help. The tour started in Hawaii and they would tour off and on until May of the next year. Here was a group who pretended to be a band, having to actually be a band. Micky had learned enough about playing the drums to fake it in front of the television cameras, but now he had to be able to really play.

It was stressful. I don't think he would have had to really worry much about it. At their first concert in Hawaii, over 8000 screaming fans greeted them when they burst onto the stage. I doubt if anyone could hear the music anyway. The concert was a big hit with the fans and with the press and put to bed, at least for a while, the rumors that the Monkees didn't play their own instruments.

From the end of December of 1966 until May of 1967, they went on a 12-city tour all over the United States. They had to travel and perform on weekends because they needed to be in the studio during the week, taping the next episode of the TV show. Davy Jones later said that they weren't really that good, but nobody cared. They did their best, and it turned out pretty good. The January 21, 1967 concert in Phoenix, Arizona was recorded and part of it was broadcast as the final episode of the first season of the show. The episode, named "The

Monkees On Tour," can be seen on YouTube and about half of it is sort of a documentary showing the guys doing silly things and just being themselves. The second half is the concert and the screaming is so loud that it's really hard to hear the music and the vocals. Davy Jones is introduced as the world's best looking midget. But, like I said, nobody cared. It was the Monkees.

At the end of the episode, Michael thanks the Rolling Stones, the Mamas and the Papas, and the Lovin' Spoonful. Then he says, "Most of all, I'd like to thank the Beatles for starting it all up for us." If nothing else, the Monkees were a class act.

"I'm a Believer"

To prepare for their second album, Kirshner wanted to bring in other talent besides Boyce and Hart, so they decided to take the whole musical operation to New York and record there. Therefore, the boys flew back and forth filming the show and recording their next album. Kirshner knew a relatively new singer from his work at the Brill Building in New York named Neil Diamond. Diamond was just getting started and had had one hit with "Cherry Cherry." He had written another song called "I'm a Believer," and Kirshner wanted that song for the Monkees but Diamond was reluctant to give it up. Diamond wanted to retain half of the rights to the song, but Kirshner finally got his way, and they came to an agreement. The Monkees had their second hit single.

"I'm a Believer" peaked at number one on the Billboard charts, making it the group's second number one in a row. It was a two-sided hit with the B-side "(I'm Not Your) Steppin' Stone" also peaking at number twenty. "I'm a Believer" spent seven weeks at number one at the end of 1966 and the beginning of 1967. It became the biggest hit of 1967 and ended up selling over ten million copies. There are fewer than 40 singles in the entire history of music that have sold more than ten million copies and "I'm a Believer" is one of them.

The double-sided hit was included on the second Monkees album called *More of the Monkees* and, of course, it went right to number one. In fact, it was the album that bumped their first album *The Monkees* out of the number one spot. *More of the Monkees* would spend eighteen weeks at the top meaning that the Monkees held the number one spot for 31 consecutive weeks in 1966 and 1967.

More of the Monkees was just that: more of the same treatment they had received on the first album. They were kept out of the loop so completely that when the album was released, the group was on tour and didn't know about the album until after it had been released to the public. Again, the guys were used only for their vocals. Either Micky or Davy sang lead vocals, and they would also sing backup vocals on several songs along with Peter on two songs. Peter is not shown playing an instrument on any of the tracks of the album, except one and neither is Michael Nesmith. Michael did write two of the songs and appears as the producer on a couple, one of which ("Mary, Mary") shows Peter Tork playing the guitar, the only song on which he does so.

Other than the few exceptions, the album was written by other people and performed by other people. When the guys got a chance to actually see the physical album and read Don Kirshner's liner notes, they became furious. Kirshner talked about the writers and then toward the end of the liner notes, casually mentioned, almost as an afterthought, that the Monkees themselves had participated in the project.

Michael was ready to go on strike. No, it was worse than that. The boys were furious. He filed a complaint with Rafelson and Schneider and demanded that the four of them be allowed to record their own music. I find it appalling that no one could understand what the boys were feeling. The powers that be treated them like they were employees who should just take their paycheck and shut up, but the guys viewed themselves as musicians first and actors second.

Michael demanded artistic control over future recordings. Kirshner couldn't understand why they were upset. They had gotten paid, hadn't they? The public was happy, the production company was happy. Why weren't the Monkees happy? But, what could they do? The Monkees were the hottest property in the country, and it meant a lot of money if they were to walk off the set and break their contracts, so Rafelson and Schneider did the only thing they could do: they fired Don Kirshner.

THE REVERSE BRITISH INVASION

OK, that did not happen right away. Much more drama was to occur before Don Kirshner was shown the door. During the lull after the concert tour and before the next album would be recorded, the boys took the opportunity to visit England. They didn't go together, but each went separately. Davy Jones, was, of course, British, and he caused almost as much a stir as the Beatles did in their homeland. The girls screamed, and Davy took it all in. The Monkees were very popular in England, perhaps second only to the Beatles. Certainly, they were the most popular American group at the time, and Davy was the favorite of the four. He was so popular that another British performer who happened to have the same name (he went by the name David Jones) decided to change his professional name to David Bowie.

Micky Dolenz also went to England and got to meet Paul McCartney personally. He even spent some time at Paul's house. Micky thought that the members of the Beatles saw the Monkees as competition, but that was not true. The Beatles were fans of the Monkees themselves and enjoyed their records just like the rest of the world. Micky was even invited to sit in on a recording session with the Fab-Four as they recorded "Fixing a Hole" which would appear on the future *Sgt. Pepper's Lonely Hearts Club Band* album. But, the most important thing to happen to Micky while he was in England was during the taping of the TV show *Top of the Pops*, where he met a British girl named Samantha Juste.

Micky fell immediately. It was truly love at first sight, and it appeared the feeling was mutual. When Micky returned to the States, she was all he could think about. He wrote a song about Samantha called "Randy Scouse Git" which in British slang means "horny Liverpool bastard." The song made it clear that he was head over heels in love.

Legends of Rock & Roll – The Monkees

Some say that this is the best song Micky ever wrote. Samantha Juste would, in 1968, become the first Mrs. Dolenz.

It would be the final nail in the coffin that was the relationship between the Monkees and Don Kirshner. While Micky was gone to England, Kirshner brought the band into the studio to record a new song from his favorite song writer, Neil Diamond. Davy was the only Monkee in town and he was brought in to sing vocals. The record they recorded was "A Little Bit Me, A Little Bit You." The flip side started out to be another Neil Diamond song called "She Hangs Out" and a disc of the two songs was actually manufactured.

When Michael returned to America (he, too, had gone to England during the break), he found out what Kirshner had done and in a meeting between him and Kirshner and some others, threatened to leave the group. Kirshner just would not back down. He saw the Monkees strictly as a tool to make money. He didn't see them as four individuals who wanted some say in their own future.

The fact that Kirshner had, in effect, gone over everyone's head and shipped the original record to Canada was reason enough to know that he was just out for himself. He did not have the group's interest at heart. He was just interested in the money machine that he had created, and he didn't care if the actual members of the group did the work or not, just so a record was made and the money kept rolling in. This did not sit well with the Monkees, obviously, but it also did not sit well with Rafelson and Schneider. They called Kirshner in and told him he was done. Clean out your desk and leave. Don Kirshner no longer had his money machine.

Michael had previously recorded his own song in defiance of Kirshner and when the new producers, Lester Sill and Emil Viola took over, they replaced "She Hangs Out" with "The Girl I Knew Somewhere" (with Micky Dolenz as lead singer) for the B-side of "A Little Bit Me, A Little Bit You." Except for Canada where the original record was released, that's what went out to the public. I suspect if you live in Canada and have a copy of that original record, it is worth quite a bit by now. This was the first song written by a Monkee to appear on a record.

"A Little Bit Me, A Little Bit You" came out in March of 1967 and quickly rose to number two on the Billboard charts. (The public, at the time, had no idea what was going behind the scenes.) The only Monkee who performs on the record is Davy Jones. There is a rumor that the background singing was done by Neil Diamond himself, although I cannot verify that. They had their second two-sided hit when "The Girl I Knew Somewhere" just cracked into the Top 40, peaking at number 39. "A Little Bit Me, A Little Bit You" was not part of any album. It did not appear on any album until years later when Colgems was putting together a *Greatest Hits* album and included it.

Of course, there was some legal wrangling as a result of the firing. Kirshner sued Screen Gems, and Screen Gems sued him back. They eventually settled out of court for an undisclosed sum of money, but Kirshner's career would never be the same. If he had tempered his ego a little and given the boys more credit and not treated them like some sort of commodity, he might have stayed with the group for years and made much more money.

In 1967, we were getting into Vietnam in a big way. The draft was being enforced like never before. I had already served four years in the Air Force and so didn't have to worry about it, but the four Monkees sure did. Rafelson was visioning a repeat of the scene when Elvis had to join the Army and had all of his hair cut off. What would the draft do to the Monkees?

As it turned out, nothing. Davy got out of the draft because he was the sole support for his father. Michael had already served in the Air Force (like me) and so was exempt. Micky had had some sort of childhood illness that got him exempted and, believe it or not, Peter told the draft board that he was gay. In those days, that would keep you out of the military. It was a little white lie (Peter is not gay), but they excused him from having to worry about it.

"Headquarters"

When season one ended, the boys had a break before they were required to start on season two. Thankfully, they were renewed despite weak ratings. The guys could have gone on vacation and relaxed, but they were determined to record an album on which they played the music. That was very important to them, and I think you can understand why.

Consequently, the spring of 1967 was spent rehearsing and recording *Headquarters*, which would be their third album, but the first which was really recorded by the four Monkees. They asked Chip Douglas to produce the album, taking over Don Krishner's post. Douglas was a musician himself and, eventually, they asked him to contribute to the album. The guys didn't write all of the songs on the album, but they did play on every one. The album was released on May 22, 1967 and shot right to number one on the Billboard charts. It sold 2 million copies in the first two months and by 2008, its sales were at 11.6 million. In 2005, a man named Robert Dimery wrote a book called "The 1001 Albums You Must Hear Before You Die". *Headquarters* is included in that list.

As popular as the album was, there was not a single hit that came from the album. The music was great and the fans loved it, but the singles that were released just did not perform. The boys were unaffected. They would get it the next time.

During the recording of *Headquarters*, the Emmy Awards were held for the previous year of television. The show won "Outstanding Comedy Series." Jim Frawley also won Best Director for the episode, "Royal Flush". In his acceptance speech, he tried to make a joke but it just ended up letting the boys know that they still were not respected in the industry. He said that the award was due to "four very special guys," and then he said "Harpo, Chico, Groucho, and Zeppo." I think it was meant to be a joke, and all four boys laughed, but I read that the boys were very insulted. Maybe they were keeping their feelings inside. The "Outstanding Comedy Series" went to the producers of the show, and when Rafelson and Schneider came to the stage to accept the award (from Jimmy Durante, of all people), they said, "This really belongs to the Monkees." So, they, at least, recognized their achievements.

Next, they went back to work on the album. If nothing else, they were professionals and were determined to prove that they belonged to this world of popular music. Honestly, it was tough going. They had never really played together as a cohesive band without a lot of backup. It took some getting used to.

The album was finally finished and was released. A few of the tracks on the album deserve mentioning. Track four on side one is called "Band 6" and it is only 38 seconds long. It consists of a short instrumental track that includes Chip Douglas's voice saying "I think you got it Micky." The track is said to be a tribute to the old "Loony Tunes" theme song that you heard the end of most Bugs Bunny cartoons.

Another track which was more Monkees nonsense was called "Zilch." This track is just over a minute in length and consists of just voices speaking sentences over and over. It doesn't make any sense and it wasn't meant to. This was the Monkees, and they had their reputation to uphold.

Two of my favorite tracks on the album are "Shades of Gray" written by Barry Mann & Cynthia Weil. This is a haunting ballad which shows Davy's vocal work to its best. The other is a song that if it were released in the late Fifties, probably would have been a big hit. "No Time" sounds a lot like the songs of Little Richard in the Fifties. Peter is pounding the piano and Micky does the vocals. Being a Fifties person, I really enjoyed this song.

Headquarters only spent one week at number one being knocked out, ironically, by the Beatles *Sgt. Pepper's Lonely Hearts Club Band* which dominated the summer of 1967. In England, they released the song "Randy Scouse Git" which you'll remember is slang for words that British radio did not want to say on the air. (This was the Sixties, after all.) So, Micky Dolenz (who wrote the song) came up with the idea of calling the song "Alternative Title" and that's what the song was known as in England. It was a big hit there, peaking at number two on the British charts.

After the album was finished, the boys needed to go on tour and promote it. They started at the Hollywood Bowl and playing in front of a live audience, proving once and for all that they were playing their own instruments and, yes, it was really them on the songs on the album. Part of the tour was the foolishness that had become the trademark of the Monkees. They jumped and ran around the stage and did crazy things. Every night it was different because the boys would do whatever they felt like doing at the time. It was a concert like few had ever seen before.

The band was one of the first to use psychedelic lights to heighten the experience. Later, this would become a staple of many bands. The summer was spent mostly touring, going to cities like Los Angeles and New York.

"Pleasant Valley Sunday"

The next day after the Hollywood Bowl concert, the band was in the studio to record their next single, "Pleasant Valley Sunday." The song was written by the legendary husband-wife team of Gary Goffin and Carole King. The name comes from a street in West Orange, New Jersey called "Pleasant Valley Way" where the two were living at the time.

"Pleasant Valley Sunday" peaked at number three on the Billboard charts and went to number eleven in England. Even though the song was released in the summer of 1967, it was featured in two of the episodes in season two: "The Picture Frame" which was the second episode of the season and "Monkee Mayor" which was the fourth.

The flip side of "Pleasant Valley Sunday" was a hit as well. "Words" was an original Boyce and Hart song that had appeared on the *More of the Monkees* album and featured Micky as the lead singer. This time, however, it was the Monkees themselves that were playing the instruments. The record became a double-sided hit as "Words" peaked at number eleven.

With the start of the second season, they needed another album. *Headquarters* had done well but wasn't the success they were looking for. They decided to go back to the pop sound of the first two albums, only this time, they had control of the music. While recording season two, they travelled to Paris to film the episode "The Monkees in Paris." Most of France had never heard of the Monkees, and their antics didn't go over well with the French people.

Traveling to London, after shooting finished in Paris, was another story. The people in London loved the Monkees, and the group had had several hits there. Plus, the people remembered them from the earlier trips they had made. They were able to hob-nob with rock and roll royalty in London, going to parties where members of the Beatles, Rolling Stones, and The Who attended. They mingled with them all. Most of these guys loved the Monkees.

Back in the states, they started work on their fourth album which would be called *Pisces, Aquarius, Capricorn & Jones Ltd.* Now for astrology fans out there, you can probably figure out the meaning of the title. Micky is a Pisces, Peter is an Aquarius, and both Michael and Davy are Capricorns, so rather than repeat the sign, they just used Davy's name.

The album was released on November 6, 1967 and contained just the one hit, "Pleasant Valley Sunday." The album itself became their fourth number one album in a row. Unfortunately, it would also be their last number one. Yes, 1967 was their best year. Things began to decline after that.

Pisces, Aquarius, Capricorn & Jones Ltd. contained two tracks in which Micky played the Moog Synthesizer. Micky has been called a gadget freak and whenever anything new came out that he thought was cool, he bought it. He purchased one of the first Moog synthesizer's shortly after they became available to the public. A couple other albums had featured the Moog earlier in 1967, but *Pisces, Aquarius, Capricorn & Jones Ltd.* was among the first. The two songs that feature the Moog are "Daily Nightly" and "Star Collector." Every song from the album was used on the television show except two. The songs skipped were "Hard to Believe" and "Peter Percival Patterson's Pet Pig Porky" both from side two.

The other song of note on this album is "What Am I Doing Hangin' 'Round?" which is a real country sounding record. It was co-written by Michael Martin Murphy, so it's easy to see that this is a country song. Michael sings lead on the song, and he liked the song because he saw the future of the Monkees to be in a country direction. Of course, no one else felt that way.

Also, a song of note is "Cuddly Toy" which is a fairly risqué song by Monkee standards. It was written by Harry Nilsson who just a year or so later would begin his own singing career with "Everybody's Talkin.'" Harry Nilsson, known as just Nilsson had a very successful career during the Seventies writing his own songs and writing for others.

"Daydream Believer"

The next single for the group was "Daydream Believer", a song written by John Stewart who was, at the time, an ex-member of The Kingston Trio. The song was recorded at the same time as the *Pisces, Aquarius, Capricorn & Jones Ltd.* album but didn't make it on that album. Instead, they saved it for the next album called *The Birds, The Bees & The Monkees*.

At first, even though Davy sings lead on the song, he didn't like it. He did not want to sing it and if you listen carefully, you can hear a little annoyance in his voice. But, later, when the song went to number one in the United States, he tempered his opinion and decided it was an OK song, after all.

John Stewart had written the line "You once thought of me as a white knight on a steed. Now you know how funky I can be." Davy changed the word "funky" to "happy." The song reached number one in December of 1967 and stayed at the top for four weeks. "Daydream Believer" and the album *Pisces, Aquarius, Capricorn & Jones Ltd.* were both number one at the same time, so the Monkees held down the top position on both the singles chart and the album chart. This is not unheard of (the Beatles did it several times), but it is relatively rare. It peaked at number five in the United Kingdom. Unfortunately, this would be the last number one the guys would ever have, but "Daydream Believer" is a classic. I find myself singing along to it every time I hear it. It is truly one of the Monkees' best songs.

In 1979, Anne Murray would record the song and hit number three on the Country chart and number twelve on the pop charts. I heard her version on the radio just a few days ago and I had to think a minute. Hey, this isn't the Monkees? Then I realized that Anne Murray had covered the song, and I knew right away what I was listening to.

Another example of just how good 1967 was for the group, Linda Ronstadt, at the time a member of The Stone Poneys, recorded a song written by Mike Nesmith. "A Different Drum" was a fairly big hit, reaching number thirteen on the Billboard charts. But most importantly, it legitimized Mike as a song writer and it kicked off Linda Ronstadt's career which would become as big as it gets over the next twenty years or so.

In 1967, the Monkees were on top of the world. They had a hit (sort of) television show. They were consistently hitting number one on the charts. They were partying with the Beatles and touring with Jimi Hendrix. They were millionaires and flying in their own private jets. What more could you ask for?

1968 would be a totally different story.

A HOUSE OF CARDS

I'm sure you understand that the four Monkees were not really friends. This band was not put together like traditional bands. It didn't start with four people who knew each other or grew to know each other as the band progressed. These guys were relatively strangers when they met and they were four completely different personalities.

In 1968, this began to become much more prevalent. Michael was a private person and felt he was the only true musician among the group. He really didn't want much to do with the other three, so he holed up in his home and wrote music and played and pretty much ignored everyone else. This would not only hurt his professional life, but his private life as well. His marriage to Phyllis was falling apart. They would later divorce in 1972, but that is still in the future.

Peter played the bumpkin on the TV show but in real life, he was a very intelligent person. Peter has been compared to Ringo Starr on the television show. He acted silly and was, sometimes, the butt of the joke. If I had to compare the four Monkees to the four Beatles, I would say that Peter is more like George Harrison in real life. Peter was a loner like Michael, but he was into Hare Krishna and he experimented with all of the popular drugs of the Sixties.

Micky and Davy were the most outgoing of the four. They didn't try to hide behind walls in their homes but went out and met the public. Davy was rumored to be going out with various women, Sally Field among them but Davy only had eyes for one girl at that time: a girl he met in Hawaii named Linda Haines. He and Linda were married, secretly, in 1968. It was kept a secret for about eighteen months and when the fans found out, they were not happy. Davy had always portrayed this happy-go-lucky ladies' man, and his fans held on to the belief that he might fall for one of them. Davy and Linda would have two daughters: Talia Elizabeth (born October 2, 1968) and Sarah Lee (born July 3, 1971). They divorced in 1975.

Micky spent time with his friend from England, Samantha Juste. Unlike Davy, this relationship was out in the open. Juste even moved to the U.S. so she could be with Micky.

The boys had started out as strangers and, it seemed, a year of working together on the show had not really changed that much. Now that they were recording their own music, they drifted even further apart. Each member of the group would come in and record his portion of a song, sometimes using his own session musicians. They didn't even see each other when they recorded. *Pisces, Aquarius, Capricorn & Jones Ltd.* was pretty much done this way.

Things were starting to unravel, and producer Chip Douglas wasn't sure how to fix it. And it was getting worse. The second season was more of the same, and the guys were getting tired of it. The scripts seemed stale, and it was as if they were just doing the same thing over and over. Which they were.

They tried to mix it up a little by inviting guests in to be on the show. They wanted to make it more of a variety show than the situation comedy that it had been. They brought in Frank Zappa and some other musicians to guest on the show, but it didn't seem to make any difference. The ratings didn't improve, and the network was tired of fighting the guys at every turn.

In February of 1968, the word came down from on high that the show was cancelled. They had produced 32 episodes in the first season, but the second season fell short of that with just 26 episodes to make 58 total. I believe all of them can be found on YouTube. Some say that the last twelve episodes or so of the series were their best. The network knew that they were running toward the end and pretty much let them have all the freedom they desired in the filming of the show. Some really great stuff came out of those last twelve episodes. However, it wasn't enough. The public had gotten tired of the antics, and the show sputtered to an inglorious end.

Proof of the quality of these last shows is that episode number 52, "The Devil and Peter Tork" was nominated for an Emmy Award. That, also, was not enough to keep it going. A list of episode titles is included at the end of this book, so you can use that to find a favorite episode if you would like to watch one.

"The Birds, The Bees & The Monkees"

In April of 1968, the band released their fifth album *The Birds, The Bees & The Monkees*. This was the album that broke their number one streak on the Billboard charts. *The Birds* only peaked at number three which anyone else would kill for but which was a setback for the group. The album is an odd one. It features each of the members of the band, but never (or hardly ever) together.

There are twelve songs on the album, but only three of them contain work by more than one member of the band. "Daydream Believer" was, of course a big hit, as I've discussed, and all four of the group play on the song. However, "Valleri", which was their next hit, peaking at number three on the charts, has the lead vocal by Davy Jones, but no other member of the band plays on the record. Both of these songs had been recorded almost a year earlier. "Valleri" had been recorded for season one of the television show, but that version was never released to the public. In late 1967, it was re-recorded and the brass instruments were added.

I like the story of how "Valleri" was written. Boyce and Hart were commissioned to write a song with "a girl's name" for the group. They tried every name they could think of and just couldn't come up with anything. The morning they were to debut the song (this was when Don Kirshner was still around), Kirshner called and asked if they were ready to audition the song. Yes, they said, we sure are, knowing they had nothing. In the car on the way to the audition, Boyce and Hart came up with the name "Valleri" and the distinctive chords you hear during the song. That was enough to sell it to Kirshner. I guess they worked better under pressure.

The other two songs which contain more than one Monkee are "Auntie's Municipal Court" which features Micky as lead vocal and Mike Nesmith as backing vocals and guitar and "Zor and Zam" which features Micky, again as lead vocal, with Davy and Mike as backing vocals. Those are the only songs which are collaborations of more than one member of the group. Every other song could be called a solo performance for that particular person.

The main problem was that each member of the group wanted to play a different style of music and if you listen to *The Birds, The Bees & The Monkees*, you can hear that. Davy was a showman and had worked in Broadway Theater. He leaned toward show tunes. Michael was into Country & Western and the weird psychedelic types of music. I find it interesting that he was interested in such diverse styles. Micky was a rock and soul man. Peter was a serious musician despite how he performed on the show. He had submitted several songs for the album, but none of them were accepted. The only time we hear Peter on the album at all is when he plays the piano during "Daydream Believer."

The wedge between the members of the Monkees was growing wider and wider.

After "Valleri," the record company released a single which was not attached to any album at the time. "D.W.Washburn" was released on May 27, 1968 and was a so-so hit, peaking at number nineteen on the Billboard charts. It was the first Monkees' song not to break into the Top Ten, and it signaled a decline that would only end with the demise of the Monkees. It did a little better in England hitting number seventeen, but in Canada, it was a big hit, peaking at number two. The song was written for the Coasters who recorded it in 1967 long after they had faded from popularity. It was written by Jerry Leiber and Mike Stoller, a famous writing team who penned much of what the Coasters recorded. I consider them to be one of the best writing teams this country has ever produced. The song was not a hit for the Coasters, but the Monkees did pretty well with it.

"Head"

Free of the series, they decided to do what the Beatles had done: make a movie. They started work on *Head* which was a deliberate attempt to imitate the Beatles style of stream of consciousness storytelling. It has been called a psychedelic adventure comedy film musical. Still attached to Rafelson and Schneider, the former directed the movie and the latter was executive producer. Rafelson also acted as co-producer and co-writer along with a relatively unknown actor named Jack Nicholson.

The movie was filmed with the working title *Changes* but was later changed to *Head*. The term "head" refers to someone who smokes pot. The film featured a number of guest appearances or cameos by other actors who were well known at the time. Victor Mature had a role as did Annette Funicello and Jack Nicholson. There were other cameos from people like the former boxing champion Sonny Liston. Raybert Productions was also working on another little film called *Easy Rider* which Nicholson had a part in, so they brought over Dennis Hopper who also appears briefly in the movie.

Head was screened by test audiences in August of 1968 and the response was so bad that they cut the movie from 110 minutes down to 86 minutes. This shorter version was released to the public on November 6, 1968. The response was immediate, and it was all bad. The people who liked the television show didn't like the movie, and the people who didn't like the show didn't bother to go see it.

The movie was made on a shoestring budget to begin with, costing about $750,000 to produce and film. The film made back about $16,111. I think Raybert Productions would have been out of business if they hadn't recouped their losses with *Easy Rider* which, of course, was a gigantic hit.

Legends of Rock & Roll – The Monkees

One of the reasons the movie failed (besides the fact that it just wasn't a very good movie) was that Jack Nicholson had written the script while under the influence of marijuana. It is rumored that most of the boys were high during much of the filming of *Head*.

Head was the first movie to be promoted without mentioning who played in the movie. There were a great many people who went to the theater no knowing who actually starred in the movie. As soon as the Monkees appeared on the screen, a great many of them just got up, walked out, and demanded their money back. The word is that if the Monkees career wasn't over before the movie, it was now.

Another reason for the failure was this was 1968. It might not seem like that would make much difference, but 1967 was a happy year, for the group and for the country, generally. 1968 was an entirely different matter. Civil rights protests had begun. Martin Luther King, Jr. was assassinated in April and just two months later in June, Robert Kennedy was killed. America was not in the mood for the type of foolishness that the Monkees produced. It was a somber time, and I think the people resented the Monkees for trying to lighten it up a little.

People were listening to Iron Butterfly and Steppenwolf and The Doors and Jimi Hendrix. None of that was really happy music. It was drug laden and serious. Bubblegum was over and with it went the Monkees.

And there are people who believe the movie was meant to fail. Rafelson and Schneider were going in a different direction. Raybert Productions would soon release *Easy Rider* and then go on to do *Five Easy Pieces*, both of which starred Jack Nicholson and both were huge successes. They were moving in a completely different direction, and the Monkees were not part of that future. What better way to cut them loose than to destroy their careers?

Only one song was released from the soundtrack of Head, "The Porpoise Song" actually came out in October, before the film, but it only reached 62 on the Billboard charts. It's a shame that the soundtrack didn't do better because it had some of the best Monkee music they had ever made.

Even though the movie bombed, it did go on to become something of a cult hit. It is certainly looked back on today with fondness. Rex Reed, a famous movie critic who was active in the late Sixties (and since), said he thought it was the greatest rock and roll movie ever made. Obviously, some people liked it.

The movie came out in November. In December, Peter Tork quit the band.

"33 1/3 Revolutions per Monkee"

One thing remained to do, however. They were under contract to film a sixty minute television special which was called *33 1/3 Revolutions per Monkee*. As usual, this is on YouTube and you can watch the whole hour long spectacle. I'm not sure what they had in mind when they wrote and produced this, for lack of a better word, "mess."

After you get past the first five minutes, it's not too bad. It really gets good at about the 30-minute mark when they do a tribute to the Fifties. Special guests Fats Domino, Jerry Lee Lewis, and Little Richard all play a couple of their hits. To me, this was the best part of the show.

Then Peter comes on and does a keyboard solo which is way too short and the band segued into a performance of what was really their last hit in the Sixties, "Listen to the Band." The song was written by Michael Nesmith and to me, comes closer to sounding like the Beatles than anything the Monkees did. It is a great song and shines a light on Mike which tells me they might have paid more attention to him during their good years as a contributor to the band. It's too bad that the song turned into something of an incoherent jam session as part of the closing minutes of the special. It left the show with everyone wondering, what just happened? I think it was a sour note to end the career of what was, a great band.

The song was not a big hit, however, only peaking at number 63 on the charts. This would be the last time the Monkees appear on the charts at all until 1986, seventeen years later.

33 1/3 Revolutions per Monkee was held by NBC for more than six months before they finally aired it. When they did, on April 14, 1969, they put it on opposite the Academy Awards, thus guaranteeing it would be seen by the least number of people. This was certainly the final nail in the coffin.

33 1/3 Revolutions per Monkee was also the last appearance of Peter Tork with the group for many years as he announced that he was leaving. It was said publicly that Peter was leaving to start his own band, but everyone knew the real reason. He just couldn't take it anymore. The remaining three struggled on without him.

Colgems had them under contract, and they were required to produce three more albums, but their hearts just weren't in it. The first of these came out in February of 1969 and was called *Instant Replay*. The album managed to break into the Top 40 and stopped at number thirty two. One single was released from the album, "Tear Drop City" but it failed to make the Top 40.

Most of the music from *Instant Replay* was taken from the vault and recorded years earlier. Even though Peter had left the group, he appears on one of the songs "I Won't Be the Same Without Her." The cover of the album only shows the three, leaving Peter out completely.

I have to give them credit. They tried to keep it together, they really did. But, nobody was interested anymore. They started touring and got weak response. Some venues actually cancelled the show because of weak ticket sales. They tried appearing on television shows. They appeared on the *Grand Ole Opry* with Johnny Cash, but that didn't really work. They even appeared with Johnny Carson on the *Tonight Show* but actually made such a bad impression that their reputation was hurt by it, rather than helped.

It took less than a year for it to fall apart again. Michael Nesmith's last album as a Monkee was their next album *The Monkees Present* in which the song "Listen to the Band" appears. This could be called the first truly Monkees album. Of the twelve songs on the album, seven of them are written or co-written by one of the remaining three. This is a really good album and it deserved to do better than it did. Unlike *Instant Replay*, this was mostly new music and showed what the guys could really do. Unfortunately, the public only remembered the old

Monkees and the album peaked at number 100. The only single "Good Clean Fun" written by Michael got as far as number 82 on the Billboard charts.

We continue to talk about final things. It makes me sad just to write this. We had already lost Peter. On November 30, 1969, Michael gave his last performance with Micky and Davy. He, too, had had enough. He left the group and started another band, "First National Band." It cost him over $100,000 (I read the number could be much larger than that) to get out of his contract with Screen Gems, but Michael later said it was worth it. He had been preparing for this for months and had written a number of songs which were meant to be sung by him as a solo artist. Now, he had his chance.

One more album was required to satisfy the Colgems contract, so the record company pulled out some material that was written by Andy Kim and Jeff Barry. Barry was hot that year, having penned the hit "Sugar, Sugar" for the Archies which was the number one song of the year in 1969. The material was basically throw away songs that no one else wanted. The album was called *Changes* after the name that was originally used for the name of the movie *Head*. A song by that same title was written for the movie but put into mothballs and not released until the Nineties. Strangely, they could have used the song on this album but didn't.

The only single released from this last album was "Oh My My" which was written by Barry and Kim. Don't confuse this song with the same song by Ringo Starr. They are totally different songs. It barely cracked the Hot 100, peaking at number 98. The album did so poorly in initial release that only a limited run of copies was made, thus making the album fairly rare. Today, the original vinyl is listed on Amazon as "unavailable", so I have no idea what it might be worth. There are, of course, cheaper remakes if you want to get the album to listen to it.

THE IN-BETWEEN YEARS

From 1970 until about 1986, nothing much happened for the Monkees. They each tried to establish solo careers, but only Michael was reasonably successful. The "First National Band" did fairly well. His band is called "country-rock" but a search of the country singles listing doesn't show any hits by the band or by Michael, so he must have not charted. Yet, I remember him, and I remember the band. He recorded three albums for the "First National Band" which he referred to as "red, white, and blue" and he considered them American standards. "Blue" was *Magnetic South* and contained Michael's only Top 40 hit as a solo artist, "Joanne." This is a country sounding song which charted on the pop charts at number twenty one but did not make the country charts. It is easily one of my favorite songs from any of the Monkees. *Magnetic South* peaked at number 143 on the Billboard Album charts.

"Red" was *Loose Salute*, which contained yet another version of "Listen to the Band." It peaked at number 159. "White" was *Nevada Fighter* which did not chart at all. "First National Band" was falling apart by this time, and it soon disbanded. Michael organized a "Second National Band" but nothing significant resulted from this.

Of the four, Michael probably had more success after the breakup than the other three. Peter did create a band called "Release" but really didn't go anywhere with it. After being rich and on top of the world in the Sixties, he and the others now found themselves broke and having to beg for scraps. They were all still young and no one had taught them how to manage money. Both Peter and Davy made bad investments on the advice of others and were soon broke. Peter had owned a castle and it was now in foreclosure. He practically became homeless, travelling from place to place looking for work.

Davy had much the same problem. He had counted on his looks all of his life and now that didn't seem to matter much. He had invested in a clothing store in New York and a mall in Los Angeles and both had gone under leaving Davy in serious financial trouble. He appeared as a guest on several television shows, usually playing himself. A famous one is the appearance on *The Brady Bunch* when Marcia makes the bold claim that Davy Jones is taking her to the prom when she had not contacted him. Davy shows up to save the day and the two attend the prom. Anyone who is a fan of *The Brady Bunch* remembers that episode.

Micky also was in trouble. He and Davy had both recorded music and released it as solo artists, but nothing was selling. They were prisoners of type-casting. Everyone saw them as a Monkee, and it seemed they could never break free of that image. Micky was also heavy into drug use. He said later that he became one of the major markets for Columbian marijuana. With little money coming in, this, of course, had the effect of draining his bank account. You may not know that Micky auditioned for the role of Fonzy on the show *Happy Days*. Of course, we all know that Henry Winkler got the job. Micky said that all the producers saw was a drummer in a rock and roll band.

Sometimes you have to hit bottom to come back. That's what happened to all four of the guys. More than the others, Peter really bottomed out. He was caught carrying drugs across the border from Mexico to Texas and spent three months in an Oklahoma jail for his crime. It could have been much worse, Peter says.

In 1976, Micky and Davy joined up with Boyce and Hart, the original writers of Monkees music, and went out on the road. Since Boyce and Hart had sung in most of the first season music for the television show, they tended to sound just like the actual group. They billed themselves as Dolenz, Jones, Boyce, and Hart and they actually recorded a self-titled album. It didn't sell much but it did wonders for the morale of the guys. They started to feel that maybe they could come back from this.

For a short time, the Monkees were hip again. People started collecting their old records. Disco was big in the late Seventies, and the Monkees seemed to fit in with that music style rather well. An album called *The Monkees Greatest Hits* was produced (they were on the Arista label by now) and did fairly well, peaking at number 58 on the album charts.

On July 4, 1976, the closest thing to a Monkee reunion occurred at Disneyland, when the four, Micky, Davy, Boyce, and Hart were joined on stage by Peter Tork. Michael, meantime, was working in a new media that he saw as the future of music. He was putting together a video to promote a song which he had done called "Rio." Music videos had been done before, but it wasn't being done on a wide basis. Michael saw it as the future and, in 1977, he filmed "Rio" (viewable on YouTube and not to be confused with the number one hit by Duran Duran done in the early 80s). The video made the rounds of several cable channels and brought Michael's name before the public. Even though the song was not a hit, it is fun to listen to. Check it out on YouTube.

Michael approached Nickelodeon television about broadcasting a half-hour show which featured music videos. He called it *Pop-Clips,* and Nickelodeon liked the idea. Consequently, the show went on the air. It was an instant hit and Warner Brothers Communications, who owned Nickelodeon, noticed the show. Building it into a bigger concept, *Pop-Clips* became what is, probably, the biggest phenomenon of the Eighties: MTV. Some people say that Michael Nesmith invented MTV. I think that is true.

In 1980, Michael's mother passed away and left him $25 million from her company, Liquid Paper. So, Michael could do pretty much anything he liked. He developed a long-form video called *Elephant Parts* which, in 1982, won the first ever Grammy for *Video of the Year*. Going back to his roots, NBC started airing his show *Television Parts* in 1985. It was a show much like the Monkees had been. Short comedy skits, intermingled with music videos. The show only lasted for the summer of 1985, but Michael was happy with it.

James Hoag

MTV REVIVES THE MONKEES

As 1986 approached, Bert Schneider realized that this was the 20th anniversary of the beginning of the Monkees. Even though Schneider could care less about the Monkees, and had abandoned them years before, he saw an opportunity to make money from them once again.

Schneider thought, what better way to get the Monkees before the nation again than to convince a cable television station to celebrate the event? Thus, he approached MTV and arranged for a showing of the original episodes of *The Monkees*. In 1986, MTV was on top of the world, and I'm not sure what it took to convince them to give up their regular programming to air *The Monkees*, but they did. On February 23, 1986, MTV, over a 22 hour period, aired all 58 episodes of the show, back to back, with only commercial breaks. In other words, they aired exactly like they had the first time.

The whole idea was a stroke of genius. MTV received the highest ratings it had ever received. (It had only been on the air for five years or so, but still, it was an enormous achievement.) It was time that a whole new generation be exposed to the Monkees.

It was easier said than done. All four had new careers of their own. Some hadn't spoken to others in years. They were never close to begin with so bringing them back together would be quite a feat. Davy was back in England playing Jesus in a production of *Godspell*. Micky was also in Britain. He was working as a director of children's programming. Peter had a new band called "The Peter Tork Project" and he was touring and while not that successful, he was making a living. Lastly, Michael, after creating *Pop-Clips* and *Elephant Parts* was now working on a new show for NBC.

Peter was the first to agree. I think he had the most to gain. David Fishof, a promoter, was hired to put the whole thing together, so he and Peter flew to England to talk to Davy and Micky. Davy thought it was a grand idea and agreed right away. Micky was a little harder to convince. He had a new career, he really didn't want to be a Monkee anymore, but Micky saw this as a chance to validate everything they had done before. The original show was criticized, and Micky thought maybe this was a chance to rectify that opinion, so he signed.

Mickey actually signed on before Davy did. Davy had tentatively signed on when he heard that Arista Records had brought Peter and Micky into the studio to record three new songs without him. The songs were to be part of a greatest hits collection called *Then & Now...The Best of the Monkees*. The songs were "That Was Then, This is Now," "Anytime, Anyplace, Anywhere," and a new version of the old Paul Revere & the Raiders' song "Kicks." Davy was not happy that he was not included in the session, but he stuck to his agreement to tour with them.

"That Was Then, This is Now" was the only hit of the three, and it was released as The Monkees, so this was the first time in over eighteen years that they were back on the charts even though it was only half of them actually on the record. The song reached number twenty on the Billboard charts. It was the last song to chart for the group.

Michael, at first, was going to join the reunion, but then decided against it. He was just too busy. He had become so successful that he didn't have time for nostalgia, and he certainly didn't need the money. Therefore, the three (without Michael) went out on tour.

They started in Atlantic City and proceeded on what was supposed to be a six-week tour. Seven months later they were still going. Nobody seemed to miss Michael. They didn't make any secret of his absence, in fact they produced a blow-up doll which looked just like Michael and put him on stage. Everyone thought it was funny. Every venue was sold out. The weird thing about this tour was that the audience consisted of both kids under eighteen who had never heard the Monkees before and their parents who remembered them well. How often can a mother and her daughter go to the same concert and both enjoy it equally well?

An interesting thing happened at every concert, though. Whenever they played the song "That Was Then, This is Now," Davy would mysteriously disappear from the stage. He refused to sing the song. No one noticed it for a while but then it became public. Asked later why this was happening, Davy said he didn't record on the song and, therefore, made no money from it, why should he sing it in the concerts?

At one of their shows in Texas, Michael Nesmith, disguised in a fat suit attended one of the concerts just to see what his old buddies were up to. He was very impressed by what he saw and, I think, for a moment regretted that he had turned them down. After the concert, he went backstage and met with the guys. This was the first time in ten years that all four of them were in the same room at the same time.

A few days later, they were playing the Greek Theater in Los Angeles when during an encore, Michael walked onto the stage. It was pandemonium. As they say, the crowd went wild. He sang two songs with the three which resulted in, what is, probably, the shortest reunion of all time. This moment became the highlight of the entire tour.

Monkee Mania lasted about two years, which is about as long as it lasted originally in the Sixties. MTV continued to play the show on a daily basis well into 1987 even repeating its 22 hour marathon of programs one more time. Old albums were re-released. Rhino Records owned most of the Monkees collection by this time and in 1987, there were seven albums on the Billboard charts at the same time. Even the album *Changes*, which didn't even dent the Top 200 albums originally now made the charts. They were gold, at least for a while. But, unfortunately, gold tarnishes.

The reunion really ended for many of the same reasons the phenomenon ended in the Sixties. The guys just didn't like each other. They could work together, sort of, but couldn't get along when in private. As the novelty of the reunion wore off and the people stopped coming to the concerts, the tension offstage became greater and greater. Once again, the Monkees were dying.

Again, they went their own ways and got back into their own projects. They got together once in a while to perform as the mood hit them. In 1989, Michael joined them once again for a couple songs at the Universal Amphitheater in Los Angeles. That was just two days before they were awarded a star on Hollywood Boulevard's Walk of Fame.

They continued to tour. In 1988, they went to Australia and in 1989, they toured Great Britain. Michael stayed home and did his own thing. Asked if he would ever join the other three, he said "probably not." The "boys" were now in their mid-forties. They had all been married twice and divorced twice. Coming into the Nineties, nothing much changed. In 1995, the three got together for a cameo in The Brady Bunch Movie which was a reunion of sorts from the Seventies television show. This time, Davy sang during the movie and Marsha was, by now, a grown woman.

It was now approaching 1996 and the 30th Anniversary of the television show. Like what happened in 1986, interest began to build once again for the group. This time, it looked like Michael might actually join them. He had had been having some financial problems as his latest project had gone wrong and the company had declared bankruptcy. I'm not sure how much he had left of the $25 million his mother had left him, but I have a feeling he needed cash.

"Justus"

On October 15, 1996, the first album in almost 30 years which included all four of the original group was released. *Justus* ("Just us") was a collaborative effort in which every song on the album was written or co-written by one of the four. No outside talent was allowed. The last time this happened was for *Head* which was in 1968.

Once again, they tried to tour. The four of them went to England, but it was a disaster right from the beginning. Here were four middle aged balding men trying to be teenagers again. It just didn't work anymore. The reviews were scathing; the concert halls were half empty.

Another movie was planned. Michael wrote the screenplay and preliminary work was being done on the movie when Davy demanded an exorbitant fee for his services to work on the movie. That was a deal breaker and the movie was shelved indefinitely. I wonder what another Monkee movie would have looked like. It's probably just as well that it wasn't made.

In 2001, the three active members (minus Michael, as usual) went back on tour yet another time, but this time the bickering was really bad. Finally, Peter said enough is enough. This time, I'm really through, and he left the band again.

This on again - off again membership made it very hard to put together a cohesive concert. This time, Micky and Davy just couldn't do it alone. They tried to tour, but the crowds were getting thinner. They received a short boost when "I'm a Believer" was featured in the movie *Shrek* in 2002, but that was short lived.

Finally, they realized that this time, it was really over. It was September of 2002. The Monkees were disbanded and each went his own way. Micky got married again, this time to girlfriend Donna

Quinter, who had been with him for some time. He got a job as a disc jockey in New York City which didn't last very long. He went back to directing and making guest appearances on several different television shows. He kept busy and felt good about his life.

Peter moved to Connecticut and joined a band called Blue Suede Blues. They played small venues in the area. It provided no pressure and enough money to make a living. Peter, too, was happy with his life. In 2009, he announced that he had been diagnosed with adenoid cystic carcinoma or in other words, throat cancer. While it worried him (who wouldn't be), Peter felt he could lick it and after therapy and several surgeries, the doctor's declared him cured. He never missed a beat, performing the whole time he was receiving treatment.

Davy continued to work at various things, getting work where he could. One of his main loves was horses. I think he always regretted not becoming a jockey like his father wanted him to. He had a farm in Pennsylvania where he kept several horses to ride and train. In 2009, he met 28 year old Jessica Pacheco and they were married. This would be his last marriage and, it seemed, this was the happiest.

Michael went back to being low-key. He retreated from public life much of the time, becoming an author. He wrote a book called *The Long Sandy Hair of Neftoon Zamora* in 1998. The book has mostly positive reviews on Amazon and appears to have been a success. He became one of the first artists to offer his music as digital downloads in the Nineties. This was a new thing back then, but, of course, an everyday occurrence today. In 2009, he published his second novel, *The American Gene*. He created a website which is operational to this day called VideoRanch and VideoRanch3D. Become a member there and keep up to date with what Michael is doing.

ONE LAST TOUR

2011 marked the 45th Anniversary of the Monkees, so another tour was warranted. It had been ten years since the last one and the people were ready to see the Monkees again. Of course, Michael would not join them, so the three went out without him. This was an unusual tour because Davy's wife, Jessica went along with them and became part of the show. This caused some discord between the three and, as usual, things did not go well.

It was the presence of Jessica that would eventually bring the tour to a halt and leave the last tour of the Monkees that included Davy Jones to end on a sour note. Jessica's brother Joseph Pacheco had been hired as Davy's stage manager and he wanted to control everything. Davy just smiled. After all, he was married to this women who was 36 years younger than he was. Life was good. Let's keep everything in the family. But the Pacheco's did not go over well with Micky and Peter. They raised such a fuss that suddenly, one day, Jessica was gone. But, her brother was still there.

On July 28, 2011, Jessica filed for divorce. On August 8, the tour suddenly came to an end and the rest of the dates were cancelled. No one knows for sure exactly what happened and it is not my place to speculate, but most feel that the Pacheco's had something to do with the cancelation.

This was the last time Davy performed with the group. He returned to his home in Florida and reconciled with his wife, Jessica and went back to living his life, at least for a few months.

Peter and Micky went back to doing what they were doing before and life went on. For everyone except Davy.

THE LOSS OF DAVY JONES

After that final tour concluded, Davy went back to his horses. They had always been his first love, and he regretted until he died that he hadn't tried his hand at being a jockey earlier in his life. On February 29, 2012, he went out on a morning ride. He had done this many times before and nothing was unusual. Except this time, when he returned from his ride, he started to feel chest pains. No one was around to help, so he went to his car to rest and wait for them to pass.

A while later, a staff member discovered him unconscious in the car and immediately called 911. He was taken to the local hospital, but nothing could be done. He might have been saved if he hadn't been alone or if he had sought help right away when the pains started. As it was, he was already dead when they arrived at the hospital. He was 66 years old. He had had a massive heart attack.

A private ceremony was held on March 7, 2012 at Holy Cross Catholic Church in Indiantown, Florida. Jessica, still Davy's legal wife, arranged the whole thing. But, in the spirit of how they left that last tour, she told the remaining three Monkees that they were not welcome at the ceremony. So, Peter, Micky, and Michael did not attend the service.

They did attend another service that they held in Los Angeles and invited all of Davy's friends who were not able or not invited to go to the one in Florida. There is no grave site for Davy. He was cremated, and I'm assuming Jessica has the ashes or spread them somewhere. So, there isn't a feeling of closure for those who knew and loved Davy Jones.

There was also a service held in Manchester, England at Lees Street Congregational Church. Davy performed in plays there when he was a child. Davy was and still is much loved in England.

I know when I heard of his death, I was saddened. I loved the music and I felt much the same way I felt when I heard John Lennon had been killed. The Monkees will never play together again. I know that death is a part of life, but it still hurts when someone goes away permanently.

Two of the people who had been so instrumental in the beginnings of the Monkees also passed away in the year before Davy. Don Kirshner, so instrumental in creating the sound that was the Monkees, passed away on January 17, 2011 and Bert Schneider, who, as one of the two guys who had started the whole thing, died on December 12, 2011.

Don Kirshner was posthumously inducted into the Rock and Roll Hall of Fame in Cleveland, Ohio, something he had wanted his entire life, but didn't live long enough to see. The Monkees, however, have not yet been admitted. I think that is a travesty. Surely, they have done as much, if not more, for the business of music in this country and just for Rock & Roll in general than some who have been inducted into the Hall.

I will always miss the Monkees. The remaining three still tour once in a while and I'm hoping they come close enough to me to see some time in the near future. Did you know that there is a Monkees Convention every year? You can travel and spend a couple days with other Monkee fans. This year (2014) it was held in Meadowlands, New Jersey on March 14, 15 and 16. Peter Tork and Micky Dolenz both came to participate. I told my wife, maybe next year, we can go.

(The next paragraph was written in 2020, when I was updating this book.)

This book was first written in 2014. Since then, we might have lost Michael in 2018 when he had a massive heart attack. He received quadruple bypass surgery which saved his life and he is still with us, today. However, in 2019 we lost Peter Tork. He died on February 21, 2019 at his family home in Mansfield, CT. I reported a few pages back that he thought he had licked the throat cancer that had afflicted him in 2009. He may have thought he did, but it wasn't true. The cancer came back at some point during that last ten years and in 2019, he died of it. Now there were only two Monkees left, but this time, both of them came to Peter's funeral. Alas, I never did get to see any of them play in person.

LEGACY OF THE MONKEES

During the year, 1967, the Monkees outsold both the Beatles and the Rolling Stones.

As of 2012, they have sold more than 65 million copies of their albums and singles worldwide.

A comic book which featured the Monkees was published from 1967 until 1969 and ran for seventeen issues. It was published by Dell Comics.

Their debut album *The Monkees* stayed at number one for thirteen weeks, a record for a debut album that would not be equaled for twenty years.

The group was awarded a star on the Hollywood Walk of Fame on July 10, 1989.

As mentioned before, Jack Frawley won the Primetime Emmy Award in 1967 for "Outstanding Directorial Achievement in Comedy" for "Royal Flush", their first aired episode. Rafelson and Schneider won Emmys that same year for "Outstanding Comedy Series." Frawley was again nominated the next year, 1968, for directing "The Devil and Peter Tork."

This is a strange one, but in 2004, TV Land network awarded *The Monkees* show the award for "Favorite Sing-Along Theme Song" for, I assume, their theme song "Hey Hey We're the Monkees."

Including Davy Jones's untimely death in 2012, Dolenz is the only member of The Monkees who has been with the band entirely since its inception.

AFTERWORD

It's sad that the Monkees had to go out like they did. I have written about many different bands from the rock and roll era of the Fifties and Sixties (and beyond). A band has a cycle, usually that they go through. They work hard at the beginning to gain a following, then they record and have a career when they are popular, and then interest wanes and they fall out of favor and disappear.

The Monkees are one band that none of that happened to. They really never paid their dues in the beginning. It can be argued that they paid them after the fact, but that doesn't really count in the field of music performers.

I hope you have gained some insight into the lives of the four guys who made up the Monkees and had a chance to go listen to some of their music while reading this. Davy has been gone eight years as I write this. He would have been 75 today (2020) if he had lived. Peter is also gone and would be 78 this year (2020) if he had lived. Of course, the other two are still alive and kicking. They actually got together and toured some cities after Davy died (yes, even Michael), so the Monkees live on.

You can contact me at http://www.number1project.com where I occasionally blog about things that interest me in the music world (mostly, the twentieth century). Go find it and read it and leave me a comment. I also have a Facebook fan page called "Legends of Rock & Roll". "Like" me and comment there, too. If you love the music as much as I do, you'll enjoy the trip. Thanks for reading.

I hope you have enjoyed this book as much as I have enjoyed writing it for you.

James Hoag

If you have liked what you read, will you please do me a favor and leave a review of "The Monkees". Thank you.

About the Author

James Hoag has always been a big fan of Rock & Roll. Most people graduate from high school and then proceed to "grow up" and go on to more adult types of music. James got stuck at about age 18 and has been an avid fan of popular music ever since. His favorite music is from the Fifties, the origin of Rock & Roll and which was the era in which James grew up. But he likes almost all types of popular music including country music.

After working his entire life as a computer programmer, he is now retired and he decided to share his love of the music and of the performers by writing books that discuss the life and music of the various people who have meant so much to him over the years.

He calls each book a "love letter" to the stars that have enriched our lives so much. These people are truly Legends.

Selected Discography

Studio Albums

1966 - The Monkees

1967 - More of the Monkees

1967 - Headquarters

1967 - Pisces, Aquarius, Capricorn & Jones Ltd.

1968 - The Birds, The Bees & The Monkees

1968 - Head

1969 - Instant Replay

1969 - The Monkees Present

1970 - Changes

1987 - Pool It!

1996 - Justus

Singles

1966 - "Last Train to Clarksville"/ "Take a Giant Step"

1966 - "I'm a Believer"/"(I'm Not Your) Stepping Stone"

1967 - "(Theme from) The Monkees"

1967 - "A Little Bit Me, a Little Bit You"/"The Girl I Knew Somewhere"

1967 - "I Wanna Be Free"/"You Just May Be the One"

1967 - "Alternate Title" (a.k.a. "Randy Scouse Git")/"Forget That Girl"

1967 - "Pleasant Valley Sunday"/"Words"

1967 - "Daydream Believer"/"Goin' Down"

1968 - "Valleri"/"Tapioca Tundra"

1968 - "D. W. Washburn"/"It's Nice To Be With You"

1968 - "She"

1968 - "Mary, Mary"/"What Am I Doing Hangin' 'Round?"

1968 - "Cuddly Toy"

1968 - "Porpoise Song"/"As We Go Along"

1969 - "Tear Drop City"/"A Man Without a Dream"

1969 - "Listen to the Band"/"Someday Man"

1969 - "Daddy's Song"

1969 - "Good Clean Fun"/"Mommy and Daddy"

1970 - "Oh My My"/"I Love You Better"

1971 - "Do It in the Name of Love"/"Lady Jane"

1976 - "Christmas Is My Time of Year"

1986 - "That Was Then, This Is Now"/"(Theme From) The Monkees"

1986 - "Daydream Believer (Remix)"/"Randy Scouse Git"

1987 - "Heart and Soul"/"MGBGT"

1987 - "Every Step of the Way"/"(I'll) Love You Forever"

EPISODE LIST

Season One

1. Royal Flush - September 12, 1966

2. Monkee See, Monkee Die - September 19, 2966

3. Monkee vs. Machine - September 26, 1966

4. Your Friendly Neighborhood Kidnappers - October 3, 1966

5. The Spy Who Came in from the Cool - October 10, 1966

6. Success Story - October 17, 1966

7. Monkees in a Ghost Town - October 24, 1966

8. Don't Look a Gift Horse in the Mouth - October 31, 1966

9. The Chaperone - November 7, 1966

10. Here Come the Monkees (pilot episode) - November 14, 1966

11. Monkees à la Carte - November 21, 1966

12. I've Got a Little Song Here - November 28, 1966

13. One Man Shy (aka "Peter and the Debutante") - December 5, 1966

14. Dance, Monkee, Dance - December 12, 1966

15. Too Many Girls (aka "Davy and Fern") - December 19, 1966

16. Son of a Gypsy - December 26, 1966

17. The Case of the Missing Monkee - January 9, 1967

18. I Was a Teenage Monster - January 16, 1967

19. Find the Monkees (aka "The Audition") - January 23, 1967

20. Monkees in the Ring - January 30, 1967

21. The Prince and the Paupers - February 6, 1967

22. Monkees at the Circus - February 13, 1967

23. Captain Crocodile - February 20, 1967

24. Monkees à la Mode - February 27, 1967

25. Alias Micky Dolenz - March 6, 1967

26. Monkee Chow Mein - March 13, 1967

27. Monkee Mother - March 20, 1967

28. Monkees on the Line - March 27, 1967

29. Monkees Get Out More Dirt - April 3, 1967

30. Monkees in Manhattan (a.k.a. "The Monkees, Manhattan Style") - April 10, 1967

31. Monkees at the Movies - April 17, 1967

32. Monkees on Tour - April 24, 1967

Season Two

33. It's a Nice Place to Visit... (aka "The Monkees In Mexico") - September 11, 1967

34. The Picture Frame (aka "The Bank Robbery") - September 18, 1967

35. Everywhere a Sheik, Sheik - September 25, 1967

36. Monkee Mayor - October 2, 1967

37. Art for Monkees' Sake - October 9, 1967

38. I Was a 99-lb. Weakling (aka "Physical Culture") - October 16, 1967

39. Hillbilly Honeymoon (aka "Double Barrel Shotgun Wedding") - October 23, 1967

40. Monkees Marooned - October 30, 1967

41. The Card Carrying Red Shoes - November 6, 1967

42. The Wild Monkees - November 13, 1967

43. A Coffin Too Frequent - November 20, 1967

44. Hitting the High Seas - November 27, 1967

45. The Monkees in Texas - December 4, 1967

46. The Monkees on the Wheel - December 11, 1967

47. The Monkees' Christmas Show - December 25, 1967

48. Fairy Tale - January 8, 1968

49. The Monkees Watch Their Feet (aka "Micky And The Outer Space Creatures") - January 15, 1968

50. The Monstrous Monkee Mash - January 22, 1968

51. The Monkees' Paw - January 29, 1968

52. The Devil and Peter Tork - February 5, 1968

53. The Monkees Race Again (aka "Leave the Driving to Us") - February 12, 1968

54. The Monkees in Paris (aka "The Paris Show") - February 19, 1968

55. Monkees Mind Their Manor - February 26, 1968

56. Some Like it Lukewarm (aka "The Band Contest") - March 4, 1968

57. The Monkees Blow Their Minds - March 11, 1968

58. The Frodis Caper (aka "Mijacogeo") - March 25, 1968

Printed in Great Britain
by Amazon